Success Recipes

Strategies for Starting a Business

Epris E. Ezekiel

Contents

Introduction

Building your ideal business might be difficult. The rewards can be enormous, but it requires a lot of effort, money, willpower, hard work, enthusiasm, and a significant leap of faith.

Considering that there are over 32 million small businesses in the United States (classified as companies with fewer than 500 employees), it is evident that these commercial endeavors did not begin simultaneously.

Additionally, depending on your exact niche market, there are some advantages to starting a business during certain seasons, even though there is no "ideal" time of year to do it.

However, several distinct components are involved in the actual formula for business success.

Start by posing some crucial questions to yourself: What is the business's mission? To whom are you offering your goods? What's your ultimate objective? How are your startup expenses going to be funded? Although you do not yet require specific answers, these inquiries will help you to think more practically about the requirements for starting a firm.

Chapter 1

Step-by-Step Procedure

The difficulty of creating anything from scratch is worthwhile.

Making bread, building a bookcase, establishing a job, and starting a family all begin with very little and culminate in amazing creations. Making anything from scratch is difficult but incredibly satisfying. The same is true when starting a business. Diddly-squat is the starting point, and with a little perseverance and creativity, you can create a game-changing concept.

But where do you start?
Yes, that is a valid question. Luckily, you've arrived at the ideal location. After researching and keeping an eye on start-ups for a few years, I have some knowledge about how to create a successful startup from nothing

more than a seed idea and passion.

We'll take you through the process of starting a business from scratch step-by-step below. We think that following a tried-and-true roadmap will increase the chances of success, even though it's conceivable to wing it and stumble onto success—there's a reason why 90% of startups fail.

But since you'll do things correctly, you won't be included in that statistic. Moreover, this book will help.

Getting started

Identify a Need

The majority of businesses fail because they begin with a great idea, service, or product. Take a step back and scratch that.

Disregard any creative fixes or revolutionary ideas. You must first identify an issue. It can be a problem that affects you, your neighbor, or a community close to you. Look for it.

Use these four techniques to get ideas for your business:

1. **Put Your Present Issues and Interests in Writing:** What problems and worries do you have at night? What would you pay a lot of money to have fixed by someone else?

2. **Look at blogs that review products:** Have you seen a product that has potential but is underperforming? Why are consumers expressing dissatisfaction (and appreciation) with

the product? Is there anything better you could do?

3. **Investigate Reddit's Niche Communities:** An invaluable resource for consumer research is Reddit. Investigate specialized subreddits to find out what is creating buzz. Observe any patterns.

4. **Look through consumer marketplaces:** Examine Online Marketplaces: Top-selling items on Etsy, eBay, and Amazon have earned their position for a reason. Examine their successful strategies, look for any gaps, and consider how you could contribute. The top-ranked items on Etsy, eBay, and Amazon did so for a reason. Examine their

successful strategies, look for any gaps, and consider how you could contribute.

All of them are the only places to start. These concepts still require validation to make sure they address issues for a wider range of clients and that they are prepared to pay for a solution. After you've identified the issue, begin formulating ideas for a service or product that addresses it.

Chapter 2

Create a business plan.

In step one, you took some time to ask yourself some questions. Now, you must write down your responses in a well-written business plan. A business plan helps you determine the direction of your firm, how it will overcome any obstacles, and what you will need to keep it running.

Before you draft your business plan, you should do the following exercises to ensure that it is realistic and functional as a roadmap for your company. You need to lay down your plans and projections to begin, but don't be scared to write down things that you believe might alter later. Your business plan can be a living document that you make changes to later. It's a good idea to revise your company strategy frequently as your situation and the market change.

Perform market research.

A key component of creating a business strategy is carrying out in-depth market research on your industry and the demographics of your prospective customers. This entails reviewing SEO and public data, running focus groups, and conducting surveys.

Understanding your industry and competitors, as well as your target customer's needs, preferences, and behavior, is made easier with the aid of market research. To better understand the opportunities and constraints in your market, competitive analysis and the collection of demographic data are advised by many small business experts.

The most successful small businesses have items or services that set them apart from the competition, which has a big impact on your competitive environment and enables you to offer potential clients something special.

Verify Your Concept

It's time to defend your business idea now that you have a strong one. Prior to investing excessive amounts of time, money, and energy in your business, it is better to make sure it has a chance from the beginning.

Thankfully, validation isn't too difficult. Listening to criticism and conducting an unbiased analysis of your business idea is the most difficult phase. You'll be all right if you do that.

To validate your idea, use the following techniques. You don't have to utilize them all.

Choose the one that best suits your needs, your sector, and your circumstances:

❖ **The Three-Step Validation Process:** Start by sending out a survey with a few questions to your target audience. Second, examine the answers to find patterns and areas of discomfort. Finally, provide your product or service in advance at a reduced price to test whether or not buyers would follow through on their commitments.

❖ **The smoke test:** We verify all of our online course concepts using this technique. Use pay-per-click (PPC) ads, email marketing, and social media to create a landing page and increase visitors. Not even a finished product is necessary yet; simply promote your concept and track the number of individuals that click the large red "Buy Now" button.

❖ **Digital Devices:** These tools can validate your business, but they are also used to validate ideas for blog posts. Share your ideas on Reddit, Instagram, TikTok, and Quora to gauge interest. When you unveil the actual product, there will likely be no interest in the idea either.

Chapter 3

Determine Your Target Audience

Your business depends on your target market. You cannot achieve this if you do not learn every single detail of their needs, wants, problems, aspirations, anxieties, and desires.

To help you identify and understand your audience, use this Guide to Defining Your Target Market:

- ❖ **Begin with specifics, then expand:** Start narrow by asking, "Who will be drawn to this product or service?" as opposed to, "Who is my target market?"
- ❖ **Examine the Market as a Whole:** Determine what is popular and what could harm or benefit your company. Being ahead of the curve is the best course

of action because your target market will be impacted by other market forces.

❖ **Cite Your Rivals:** Who are your rivals aiming for? What is their marketing strategy? Have they overlooked any important niches?

❖ **Make Use of Your Social Media Information:** For better or worse, social networking sites already gather a ton of information on your followers. Consult this data to discover their psychographics and demographics.

Further segmentation is necessary when your target market has been reduced. For instance, you should divide your audience into smaller subsections if it consists of male soccer players. You may have:

✓ Soccer players who are men and coaches
✓ Male soccer players who prefer to observe rather than participate

- ✓ Male soccer players who compete
- ✓ Male soccer players in high school
- ✓ Male soccer players who play for fun

Your target audience isn't a single, homogeneous group. Varied marketing and sales strategies would probably elicit varied reactions from these divided groups. Your ability to craft tailored messaging will increase with the degree of audience segmentation you achieve.

Build Your Audience

All right, now you have a framed picture of your target market and a verified idea. That's a terrific beginning! After that, you must start establishing an audience.

Your audience consists of people who are familiar with your brand and are prepared to buy when your product launches, such as social media followers, email subscribers, podcast listeners, phone numbers, blog readers, and potential customers.

Let's begin by increasing brand recognition. There are several inexpensive ways to make your brand identifiable, as outlined in Some Foolproof Strategies to Increase Brand Awareness. A few highlights are as follows:

1. **Get the Proper Keywords:** Wherever your audience spends their digital time, make your brand visible.

2. **Address a Challenge:** Solutions sell themselves more effectively than goods. You want your customers to imagine how your brand could make their lives better.

3. **Describe a Story:** Stories are what people remember, not products. Make your brand more than just money, goods, and features to make it bigger than life

Chapter 4

Analyze your financial situation.

Establishing a business comes with costs, so you must figure out how to pay for them. Are you able to finance your startup or will you have to take out a loan? If you want to quit your job to concentrate on your business, do you have enough money saved up to sustain yourself until you turn a profit? Learn how much it will cost to start up.

A lot of startups fail because they exhaust their funding before they make a profit. Overestimating your startup capital needs is never a bad idea because it may take some time before the business starts to generate steady income.

Analyze the break-even point.

A break-even analysis is one method to figure out how much money you need. This crucial component of financial planning aids entrepreneurs in estimating the time at which their business, goods, or services will turn a profit.

The equation is straightforward:

Break-Even Point = Fixed Costs ÷ (Average Price Per Unit − Variable Costs)

This formula is a useful tool for any entrepreneur since it indicates the minimal level of performance that your company needs to meet to stay profitable. Additionally, it enables you to pinpoint the precise source of your income so that you can adjust your production targets.

The following are the top three justifications for performing a break-even analysis:

1. **Examine the data:** Consider how many products or services you would need to sell to turn a profit.

   You ask, how can I lower my total fixed costs? How might I decrease the variable expenses per unit? How can I increase sales?

2. **Pricing a product or service:** Most people base their pricing decisions on competing items' prices as well as the cost of producing their own. What are the variable charges, what are the set rates, and how much does it cost all in all? How much do tangible products cost? How much does it cost to work?

3. **Ascertain profitability:** This is typically the top priority for every business owner.

What is the amount of money I need to make to pay for everything? Which goods and services are sold at a profit and which are not?

Be mindful of your spending.

Avoid going over budget while launching a firm. Avoid splurging on ostentatious new equipment that won't help you achieve your business objectives and know what kinds of investments make sense for your company. Keep an eye on your company's spending to make sure you're remaining on course.

"Many startups tend to spend money on unnecessary things." "When starting a business, spend as little as possible on the things that are necessary for it to grow and prosper. Once you've established yourself, you can afford luxury.

NB: Tracking your expenses can be made more efficient by using accounting software. To choose the finest platform for your needs, read our reviews of the top accounting software. Our favorite choice for small businesses is Intuit QuickBooks Online, so start with our review.

Think about your choices for funding. There are several ways to raise startup funds for your company. The amount required, available options, and creditworthiness all influence how best to obtain capital for your company. There are several ways to raise startup funds for your company. The amount required, available options, and creditworthiness all influence how best to obtain capital for your company.

1. Crowdfunding: To obtain smaller sums of money from several backers, you can also start an equity crowdfunding campaign.

In recent years, crowdfunding has benefited many businesses, and there are dozens of trustworthy crowdfunding platforms tailored to different kinds of enterprises.

2. Angel investors: An angel investor may be a good choice for startups that need a large amount of money upfront. A startup company can receive several million dollars or more from investors in exchange for a direct role in managing the company.

3. Business grants: Business grants are similar to loans, but do not need to be paid back. Usually very competitive, business grants include requirements that the company must fulfill to be eligible. Seek out grants tailored to your

circumstances when applying for a small company grant. Government grants, grants for women-owned firms, and grants for minority-owned enterprises are among the options.

4. Business loans: A business loan from a bank is a helpful place to start if you need money, but it can be challenging to obtain. Use the Small Business Administration (SBA) or another lender to apply for a small business loan if you are unable to obtain one from a bank.

Chapter 5

Pick the appropriate business bank.

Size is an important consideration when selecting a corporate bank. We suggest smaller community banks because they understand the local market and will cooperate with you according to your character and overall business profile.

"They will be more selective when lending money to small businesses than big banks, which consider your credit score. "Furthermore, local banks aim to establish a personal rapport with you and will eventually assist you if you encounter difficulties or fail to make a payment. Compared to large banks, which make decisions at a higher level, smaller banks also have the advantage of making decisions at the branch level, which can happen much more quickly.

When selecting a bank for your company, you should consider the following questions:

- ✓ What matters to me?
- ✓ Would I like to have a close relationship with a bank that is ready to assist me in any manner?
- ✓ Do I want to be seen by large banks as simply another bank account?

The best bank for your company ultimately depends on your demands. It can be helpful to put your banking needs in writing so you can focus on what you need. Set up meetings with different banks and inquire about their small company lending practices to determine which bank is ideal for your

Launch an MVP

Time to make your dream a reality. Launch a minimal viable product (MVP) quickly rather than taking months or years to improve the product.

The simplest version of your product that a consumer can utilize is called an MVP. Consider Facebook. Facebook's MVP was the original, simplified version, which was merely a basic social media network with friends and updates (imagine that) and without a marketplace, groups, video, stories, gaming, or news.

To launch better MVPs, use these three strategies:

1. **First, test your ideas:** Your MVP isn't the proof. You ought to have tested your concept before creating the final product.

2. **Adopt an MLP Mentality:** Minimum Loveable Product is what MLP stands for. Launch something your customers love instead of just a product that works.

3. **Use a Soft Launch to Go Live:** A press release and fireworks are not necessary when launching your product for the first time. Keep things light and easygoing at first.

Protect Your Brand and Business

You must now formally launch your business after developing a product MVP, business plan, and target market. Establishing a brand around your concept is the first step. A brand consists of the name, logo, website, and social media images, but it's an ongoing process that requires just as much attention as developing new products, attracting clients, and managing your staff

To help you get started, here is a selection of brand-building resources:

- ✓ Eight Infallible Methods to Raise Brand Recognition
- ✓ Tips for Small Business Branding to Outperform the Competition
- ✓ How to Create a Website in Under an Hour
- ✓ What is the Best Small Business Website Builder?
- ✓ How to Pick the Ideal Color for Your Logo: The Complete Guide
- ✓ Developing a Vibrant Business Name

There is more to keeping your company safe than just purchasing a domain name and protecting your social media accounts, but these are crucial. It's about lawfully obtaining the data you need to make sure your name, logo, and concept aren't stolen. Additionally, depending on where your firm is based, submitting accurate tax returns can shield you from lawsuits or tax debt.

The following steps must be taken to secure your business and make it official legally:

- ✓ Acquire business insurance, if required.
- ✓ Certifications or licenses from the government (if required)
- ✓ Open a bank account for your company.
- ✓ Obtain a tax identification number.
- ✓ Create a business account with the state.
- ✓ Copyright.
- ✓ Brands and trademarks

We always advise getting advice from a tax expert before registering your company.

Register with the IRS and the government.

Before operating your firm legally, you must obtain business licenses. For instance, the federal, state, and municipal governments need you to register your firm. You need to prepare several documents before registration.

Articles of incorporation and agreements for operations

You need to register with the government for your firm to be recognized officially. A corporation must have an article of incorporation document that contains the company's name, mission, organizational structure, stock information, and other characteristics. Likewise, certain LLCs will have to draft an operating agreement.

An article.

Conducting business as a DBA

You must register your business name if you do not have articles of incorporation or an operating agreement. This name might be your legal name, a fake DBA name (if you are the sole proprietor), or a name you have created for your firm. For further legal protection, you may also wish to take action to trademark your company name.

You must obtain a DBA in the majority of states. Working under a false identity as a sole proprietor or in a general partnership may require you to apply for a DBA certificate. To find out about specific requirements and fees, call or visit the county clerk's office in your area. Usually, a registration fee is required.

EIN, or employer identification number
You might need to obtain an employment identification number from the IRS after registering your business. Even while sole proprietorships without workers are exempt from this requirement, you could still wish to register for one to keep your personal and business taxes separate or to avoid any issues

down the road if you decide to hire someone. To find out if you need an EIN to operate your business, the IRS has produced a checklist. You can register online for free if you do require an EIN.

Forms for income taxes

To satisfy your federal and state income tax requirements, you must submit specific paperwork. The forms you require depend on your company's structure. For details on local and state-specific tax duties, you will need to visit the website of your state. Once everything is set up, you can submit and pay your taxes on a quarterly and annual basis with the aid of the best online tax software.

"As a licensed attorney and owner of NPL Consulting, Natalie Pierre-Louis stated that while it may be tempting to wing it with a PayPal account and social media platform if you start with a proper foundation, your business will have fewer hiccups to worry about in the long run."

Invest in an insurance plan.

Getting the proper insurance for your business is a crucial step to take before you formally start, even though you may put it off as something you plan to do later. It can be expensive to deal with situations like theft, property damage, or even a lawsuit from a customer, so you need to be sure you have the right insurance.

Most small businesses can benefit from a few basic insurance plans, but you should think about a variety of business insurance options. For instance, you will need to get unemployment and workers' compensation insurance if your company will hire people.

Although you may require additional coverage based on your industry and location, the majority of small businesses are advised to purchase a business owner's policy or general liability (GL) insurance. GL provides coverage for bodily harm, property damage, and personal injury to you or a third party.

Professional liability insurance may also be necessary if your company offers services. It protects you if you operate your business improperly or fail to take certain necessary actions.

Chapter 6

Build a team.

To launch your business, you will need to find and hire a strong staff, unless you intend to work alone. The same consideration that entrepreneurs pay to their products must also be given to the "people" aspect of their enterprises.

Your product is manufactured by people. "Your priority should be to identify your founding team, comprehend any gaps, and decide how and when to fill them. Determining the team's collaboration style is just as crucial. Clearly defining roles and responsibilities, the division of labor, how to provide feedback, and how to collaborate when people are not in the same room will save you a great deal of trouble later on.

Promote Your Goods

We've reached the marketing section at last. This is the nicest part for a lot of entrepreneurs, and it's far superior to the next step, which is selling.

Marketing covers the methods and tactics (not the same, by the way) you employ to bring your brand in front of potential buyers. It includes aspects like content marketing, advertising, social media marketing, video marketing, and e-commerce marketing.

To put your plan into action after you've decided which channels to use, review the following interviews and guides:

- ❖ **Marketing Podcasts:** Guide to Podcast Marketing
- ❖ **Marketing through Influencers:** 101 of Influencer Marketing

- ❖ **Affiliate Promotion:** The Complete Affiliate Marketing Guide
- ❖ **Marketing for E-Commerce:** How to Launch an Online Store
- ❖ **Video Promotion:** Five Steps to an Effective YouTube Marketing Plan
- ❖ **Marketing on Social Media:** Expand Your Social Media Presence
- ❖ **Content Promotion:** For Startups, the Best Content Marketing Strategy

Select your suppliers.

There are B2B companies, ranging from HR service providers to business phone system vendors, that exist to partner with you and help you run your business better. For instance, with a business phone system, you can design an IVR system to automatically route your callers to the right representatives. Third-party vendors are there because running a business can be overwhelming and you and your team are probably not going to be able to do it all on your own.

Choose wisely when looking for business-to-business partners. It's crucial to find someone you can trust because these businesses will have access to your most important and possibly sensitive business data. Our knowledgeable sources advised in our guide to selecting business partners to inquire about prospective vendors' track record with current clients, their experience in your industry, and the type of growth they have facilitated for other clients.

Almost all businesses will require certain common items and services, but not all businesses will require the same kinds of vendors. Take a look at these essential features for any kind of organization.

❖ **Financial management:** A lot of entrepreneurs handle their bookkeeping when they first start their company, but as your company expands, you can save time by hiring an accountant or selecting the best accounting software.

❖ **Receiving money from clients:** To have a cutting-edge interface for generating revenue, set up a point-of-sale (POS). Inventory management and customer management features are combined with this payment technology, which largely overlaps with credit card processing, in the best point-of-sale systems. Therefore, if you intend to sell goods rather than services, point-of-sale (POS) systems are particularly crucial.

❖ **Allowing many forms of payments from customers:** Providing a variety of payment methods will guarantee that you can close a deal in the format that works best for your target client. To be sure you're getting the greatest deal for your company, compare your alternatives and choose the finest credit card processing company. This is due to the fact that processing credit cards for small businesses is frequently a direct path to increased sales and a wider clientele.

Chapter 7

Advertise and build your brand.

Before you begin selling your goods or services, you must establish your brand and develop a following of individuals who are prepared to jump at the chance to do business with you.

- ❖ **CRM systems:** You may keep consumer data on the top CRM platforms to enhance your marketing efforts. Reaching clients and interacting with your audience can be greatly enhanced by a carefully planned email marketing strategy. You should carefully expand your email marketing contact list if you want to succeed.

- ❖ **Social media:** Spread the word about your new company on social media, and after your debut, use it as a promotional

41

tool to provide fans discounts and coupons. Your target audience will determine which social media channels are best for you.

❖ **Company website:** Create a business website and take your reputation online. A website is digital evidence that your small business is operational, and many customers use the internet to research a company. It is also an excellent method of communicating with both present and future clients.

❖ **Logo:** Use a logo on all of your platforms to make it easier for customers to recognize your business. Applying the color scheme, you choose for your logo consistently throughout your brand will help it develop a recognizable and cohesive personality that customers will find easy to relate to.

Continually add engaging, pertinent content about your company and sector to your digital assets. Too many startups view their websites incorrectly.

They view their website as an expense rather than an investment, which is the problem. That is a grave error in the current digital era. Small business entrepreneurs will have an advantage in getting off to a successful start if they recognize the importance of having a strong online presence.

Developing a marketing strategy that continues after your debut is crucial to establishing a clientele since it should continuously spread the word about your company. This procedure is equally as crucial as offering a high-quality good or service, particularly at first.

Request that clients sign up for your marketing mailings.

Ask your current and potential clients for permission to communicate with you as you develop your brand. Opt-in consent forms are the simplest way to accomplish this. You can use these forms to get in touch with them and provide more details about your company.

"People receive so many disposable emails and other messages these days that by getting them to opt into your services transparently, you begin to build trust with your customers." "These types of forms typically pertain to email communication and are frequently used in e-commerce to request permission to send newsletters, marketing material, product sales, etc. to customers."

Even more importantly, opt-in forms are mandated by law. The Federal Trade Commission's CAN-SPAM Act of 2003 establishes requirements for commercial emails, which extend beyond bulk emails to include all commercial messages, defined as "any electronic mail message the primary purpose of which is the commercial advertisement or promotion of a commercial product or service." Violations of this law can result in fines exceeding $40,000.

Sell Like an Expert

Sales. Do not be alarmed, would-be business owners. You're capable.

Ultimately, if you are unable to generate revenue, it is pointless to validate your idea, identify your niche, produce your product, and establish your brand. Thankfully, marketing your goods doesn't have to be a clumsy experience with a salesperson knocking on people's doors.

Rest assured that we also detest embarrassing

sales techniques

Scale Efficiently

Once you've begun producing money, it's time to scale your business. Scale looks different for everyone depending on their goals, expectations, and bandwidth.

Scale for one entrepreneur could mean launching new items, while scale for another might mean cutting costs and increasing revenues for existing commodities.

Recall your motivation for starting your business from scratch. Was it more leisure time or more income that you desired? Was it your desire to manage your career or to solve an issue in your community?

Chapter 8

Utilize AI Resources to Launch Your Business

Your startup has the edge it needs to take on the

industry leaders thanks to AI tools. In the fast-paced, technologically advanced business world of today, it is no more a nice-to-have but rather a need.

From branding and customer interaction to brainstorming and market research, these AI tools may expedite many parts of starting and running a business. Here are a few of our top picks for AI technologies to launch and expand your company.

Ideating

- ❖ **Gravity Write:** Contributes original ideas and inspiration to brainstorming and ideation sessions.
- ❖ **Copy.ai:** Uses artificial intelligence (AI) to produce excellent writing for a range of uses, including product descriptions and marketing.

Business Assistants

- ❖ **Go via AI:** Automates the extraction and analysis of web data, which is helpful for competitor and market research
- ❖ **Swiftly:** A flexible AI assistant made to help with scheduling and task management, among other corporate processes.
- ❖ **Mem:** AI-driven memory aid that facilitates the organization and retrieval of crucial business data.

Marketing and E-Commerce

- ❖ **Brief Script:** Helps write succinct, engaging scripts for promotional and marketing videos.

- ❖ **Printful:** Incorporates AI into print-on-demand services to support e-commerce and product customization.

- ❖ **Rizz:** An AI-driven platform for optimizing marketing strategy and customer engagement.

Audio/Video

- ❖ **Runway Machine Learning:** An AI platform for motion graphics and video editing that makes complicated video production processes easier and enables you to turn text into video.

- ❖ **Dall-e:** Video thumbnails and other visual content can benefit from this AI tool for creating unique, excellent photos and artwork.

- ❖ **Descript:** Enables AI-powered audio and video editing with features like auto transcription.

Graphic Design

- ❖ **Color Mind:** An AI tool for creating color schemes that are ideal for web design and branding.

- ❖ **Booth Artificial Intelligence:** Provides automatic photo enhancement and editing that is appropriate for marketing brochures and product photos.

- ❖ **Looka:** Creates expert logos and brand materials by fusing AI with design principles.

Editing

- ❖ **Rewriter Spin:** An AI-powered tool that improves readability and originality by rephrasing current content.
- ❖ **ChatGPT:** Offers flexible help with text editing and improvement for emails and business proposals.
- ❖ **Claude:** Provides advanced language enhancement and editing tools to improve your writing.

Conclusion
Think about an exit plan.

You should plan your exit strategy from the outset, even if your business journey is just getting started. Are you going to expand the business, sell it, and then leave? Do you want a family member to inherit it? Is the ultimate objective to acquire and perhaps retain employment? From the beginning, you should consider your end goal so that you can consciously work toward it.

"All too frequently, new business owners are so thrilled about their venture and certain that everyone will be a customer that they give themselves little to no time to plan on exiting the company. "What is the first thing you see when you get on an airplane? How to disengage from it. What are they pointing out before the movie starts when you go to see it? The locations of the exits.

"I have seen company executives much too frequently who lack three or four planned exit strategies. The company's value has decreased as a result, and family ties have even been ruined.